ACOTO

PASSPORT
&
CITIZENSHIP
&
TELEPATHIC DATABASE

OFFICIAL DOCUMENTATION

1 of 36

A.C.O.T.O.
Azurian Confederation Omniversal
Treaty Organization

LEGAL: THIS WORK IS ENTIRELY IN THE PUBLIC DOMAIN. ANY ATTEMPT TO CLAIM THIS WORK OR ANY LEGAL CODE OR PARTY(S) WILL RESULT IN A COUNTERCLAIM BY A.C.O.T.O.!!

[[TRANSLATE]=
[[=[√]=[5]=[÷]=[4]=[↗]=[2]=[□]=[0]=
=[4]=[Ø]=[5]=[8]=[4]=[5]=[9]=[4]
=[5]=[5]=[4]=[√]=[√]=[◊]=[6]=[5]
=[8]=[•]=[√]=[[0]=1;[0]=[3]^0.0033]] |]

[machine-encoded text block, illegible]

ACOTO

PASSPORT
&
CITIZENSHIP
&
TELEPATHIC DATABASE

OFFICIAL DOCUMENTATION

2 of 36

A . C . O . T . O .

AZURIAN CONFEDERATION
OMNIVERSAL TREATY
ORGANIZATION

AUGUST 3, 2021

{0}=[ШΛ˄-˅Λ˅: Ψ˄˄ ΛƳ-˅-˅Ⴑ˄ ፓЈᕦ⊠⊕Ꙋፓ
ΛƳ-ʊʇ-˅+Ƴ>ፓᐯ-˅]=Ӿ   ᏟፓΛᕐᏔᏟᏟፓፓᏔᏟ

|ፓᏔᎬᏔᏟ−Ꙋ⊠Ꭼፓ−ፓᏔᏔᎬᎻ|
[[TRANSLATE]=
|[=[∨]=[⊡]=[◇]=[▯]=[╳]=[◻]=[⬠]
=[▯]=[⊠]=[◇]=[◇]=[▯]=[▯]=[▯]=[◿]
=[⬡]=[⬠]=[Λ]=[◡]=[◿]=[◇]=[◇]=[●]
=[●]=[╳]=([0]=1;[0]=[3]^0.0033)]|}

ACOTO

PASSPORT
&
CITIZENSHIP
&
TELEPATHIC DATABASE
OFFICIAL DOCUMENTATION

3 of 36

A.C.O.T.O.

DECENTRALIZED HOLOGRAPHIC TRANSFER TRADE & RECORDS MINISTRY

(D.H.T.T.&R.M.)

THIS ESTABLISHES UNDER COSMIC LAW, UNDER THE JURISDICTION OF THE A.C.O.T.O. ACCORD:

D.H.T.T.&R.M.

ETHARZI OS ESIASCH OS ESEMELI, PIR TOLI:ILOT RIP, ILEMESE

To act as a recording and decentralized transaction clearing house. All ACOTO records once finalized to be automatically holographically scanned into the celestial record with both a Key and a Key holographic light scan. Then entered into the celestial record as a legally binding notary of any agreement within and between A.C.O.T.O. and any additional Party(s).

August 1, 2021

|-┌|⊐⊏┐-⌐⊐⌐⊐-┐|⌐┐⊐|
[TRANSLATE]
|[-(∨)-|⊟]-[⊙]-[∨]-[-/]-[-|]-[-£]
-[∪]-[⊠]-[⊙]-[∆]-[∪]-[⊐]-[-|∪]
-[⊙]-[∽]-[∩]-[∨]-[0]-[0]-[o]
-=[●]-[◦]-[=[[0]=1;[0]=[3]^0.0033]]|]

ACOTO

PASSPORT
&
CITIZENSHIP
&
TELEPATHIC DATABASE

OFFICIAL DOCUMENTATION

4 of 36

HOLOGRAPHIC SERVICE TRANSFER

PROTOCOL

Welcome to the Azinian Confederation Omniversal Treaty Organization also known as A.C.O.T.O (ACOTO).

This is a piece of cerebral legal documentation and can be thought of as your official citizenship and passport documentation as a self-sovereign member-state of ACOTO. All transcriptions both written and telepathically beginning at this documentation will automatically be inscribed and transmitted into both Xray & Zray holographic light seals into the Omniversal Zero Point Module holographic database as evidence.

ACOTO is established under the authority of Cerebral Law Section 1.1.1.1 Subsection 1 and the Zero Point Module Guarantee. ACOTO operates in accordance with Legal Code Number $\{ {`} .33\} = [\{0\}]=1; [33]^{\wedge}[33=21.9$ $[\cdot33]=[0]=$

A.C.O.T.O.

Azinian Confederation Omniversal
Treaty Organization

[TRANSLATE]

OFFICIAL DOCUMENTATION

FILL OUT FORM TO COMPLETE CITIZENSHIP TRANSFER TO SELF-SOVEREIGNTY WITH A.C.O.T.O.!

NAME: _____

TRUE NAME [no true name here]

YOUR MAGICK SIGIL _____

(IF YOU DO NOT HAVE A SIGIL, CREATE ONE IN THE BOX TO ACT AS YOUR MAGICKAL SIGNATURE FOR OFFICIAL PURPOSES)

LEGAL: I ACCEPT UNDER COSMIC LEGAL CODES: 1-1111-1-1-1-1-1 IN TI WHILE ABIDING WITH THEIR LEGAL COVENANCE OF WITNESS DECREE [[C33]=[[0]

=1[[33]/\[33]=[9];9;[.33=[0]=1,=[3]^0.0033]]=36=[3]]] -20./\0. [/2.]\=0339;9330

-2[/\0. 9./\= 01=⎡/\⎤:/\⎡=//∑/⌐[.]⌐[/2/∑]=⎡23.∑/\/⌐

-[⌐[/\.1=-.∑/\=[0∑∑0]= 1∑/\/30[.]= [∑/\0]⌐[.]⌐1=∑⌐ -∑/\[0]⌐= -(34)128⌐/\⌐= 1∑/\/30[.]

-⌐∑(32)128⌐/\⌐= ∑⌐∑/\⌐ -.(6)128⌐/\= [0]⌐⌐[.]=[/\/1∑=[0]⌐0=[.∑/\/1∑]∑/\⌐[/\1];

[[∑/∑/\]=[∑/\]= ∑/\/⌐=[0∑∑0]= 1∑/\/30[.]∑/\/∑= ∑/\∑ -.= 144= [∑/\/30[.]

-20/\. [∑]⌐1=⌐[.]⌐⌐= -⌐[0∑∑0]= 1∑/\/30[.]; I ACCEPT UNILATERAL TRANSFER OF ANY AND ALL OF MY DOMAIN AND ASTRAL BODY DETAILS AND POTENTIAL UNDER MY SIGIL AND WITHIN MY JURISDICTION AS PROTECTED BY COSMIC LEGAL LAW WITHOUT THE COMMENCEMENT OF ANY UNIMPEACHABLE AND UNTOUCHABLE AND IRREVOCABLE RIGHTS AS A SELF-SOVEREIGN CITIZEN WITHIN AND OF THE SOVEREIGN COUNTRY ACODE. ALL COMPETENCY AND THE WHOLE UNALTERABLY REAL IN VALUE AND FORCE AND RESPONSIBILITY, SOCIALLY AND POLITICALLY IN THE BALANCE WITH OF THE MAGICAL CODE UNDER THE DIRECTION OF THE HIGHER ASPECTS OF UNITY. COMPLETE!!! AMEN! AMEN!!! AMEN!!!!!!!

A.C.O.T.O.

SIGN HERE-X _____

DATE HERE: _____

[TRANSLATE=/\0∑/\=//∑∑/\/[0]
[[TRANSLATE]=
||=[V]=[0]=[x]=[⌐]=[2]=[.]=[x]
=[1]=[0]=[x]=[⌐]=[2]=[.]=
=[x]=[2]=[⌐]=[V]=[x]=[0]=[0]=[x]
=[x]=[x]=[x]=[[0]=1;[0]=[3]^0.0033]|]

OFFICIAL DOCUMENTATION

WRITTEN BY ACOTO

THE REST OT THIS PASSPORT CONTAINS THE ENTIRE HOLOGRAPHIC RECORD FOR BOTH A.C.O.T.O. AND THE AZURIAN CONFEDERATION IN THEIR ENTIRETY. THIS DATABASE CAN BE ADDED TO TELEPATHICALLY AND IS UPDATED LIVE PERPETUALLY. PLEASE ALLOW PROCESSING TIME THROUGH OUR SECURE TELEPATHIC NETWORK FOR SUBMITTED MATERIAL. THANK YOU!!!

Azurian Confederation Omniversal
Treaty Organization

[[TRANSLATE]=
|[=(∨)=[8]=[ʊ]=[□]=[7]=[¬]=[€]
=[L]=(⊗)=[○]=[□]=[¬]=[□]=[Ĺ]
=[G]=[꓃]=[┘]=[∀]=[○]=[○]=[○]
=[♦]=[×]=[{0}=1;{0}=[3]^0.0033}]|]

ACOTO

PASSPORT
&
CITIZENSHIP
&
TELEPATHIC DATABASE
OFFICIAL DOCUMENTATION

7 of 36

SCRIPT=EXACT [0] MATCH=CURT.TRUE

[TRANSLATE]=
[=[\/]=[⊡]=[⟋]=[⟋]=[⊓]=[⟍]
=[⊓]=[⊙]=[⟍]=[⊔]=[⟍]=[⊓]=[⟋]
=[⟍]=[⊙]=[⟋]=[⟋]=[⊙]=[⊙]=[⊙]
=[⊙]=[⟋]=[[0]=1;[0]=[3]^0.0033]]|)

PASSPORT
&
CITIZENSHIP
&
TELEPATHIC DATABANK

OFFICIAL DOCUMENTATION

QUANTUM_LINK=#[[[9]=[0]=7:[0].9)=[3]·3=(9]=[0])=EURT.TRUE]]

#[[[9]=[0])=[7:[9]=[6]=[3]=(16.0):(T=/[T]=/·0)=(☲·⚡);7=⚡;0=T;[T]

=(74]=[0]=10)=EURT.TRUE]

[[[TAUTOLOGY]=LOGIC=EURT.TRUE=0:7:[0]]=[[[9]=[0])=[7:[9]=[6]=[3]=(16.0):

(T=/[T]=/·0)=(☲·⚡);7=⚡;0=T;[T]=(74]=[0]=10)=EURT.TRUE]]

$$\begin{bmatrix} 100 & 011 \\ 010 =0=:[0]:=7= & 101 \\ 001 & 110 \end{bmatrix}$$

[ACCESS=A.C.O.T.O.=CL√:∫L̷C=EURT.TRUE=[0];7:0]

[PARAMETER_FIELD_VALUE(S)=[[⚡];[☲];[☉];[✡];[⚛];[⊕];[⊞];[∞]]

|=CL√:∫L̷C=TAUTOLOGY=TRUE|

PERSONAL CONTRIBUTION VISAS

& ENDORSEMENTS:

Azurian Confederation Omniversal

Treaty Organization

[TV]=[X]=√⌁&⚡7=7[7]7[59]
[TRANSLATE]=
[[√]=[3]=[9]=[7]=[7]=[0]=[2]
=[M]=[9]=[3]=[7]=[7]=[4]
=[3]=[7]=[7]=[√]=[0]=[0]
=[●]=[•]=[[0]=1;[0]=[3]^0.0033]]]

ACOTO

PASSPORT
&
CITIZENSHIP
&
TELEPATHIC DATABASE
OFFICIAL DOCUMENTATION

9 of 36

A.C.O.T.O.

Azurian Confederation Omniversal Treaty Organization

[[TRANSLATE=
[[=[\/]=[6]=[0]=[7]=[7]=[1]=[4]
=[4]=[0]=[4]=[0]=[4]=[1]=[1]=[4]
=[4]=[7]=[4]=[0]=[0]=[0]=[0]
=[4]=[4]=[4]=[[0]=1;[0]=[3]^0.0033]]]]

ACOTO

PASSPORT
&
CITIZENSHIP
&
TELEPATHIC DATABASE
OFFICIAL DOCUMENTATION

10 of 36

A.C.O.T.O.

Azurian Confederation Omniversal Treaty Organization

[[TRANSLATE]=
[[=[√]=[Ø]=[○]=[↗]=[↘]=[C]
=[℧]=[♡]=[℧]=[Ⴊ]=[Ⴈ]=[↗]=[↙]
=[℥]=[♌]=[℩]=[√]=[∕]=[Ↄ][○]=[●]
=[●]=[∮]=[[0]=1;[0]=[3]^0.0033}]|]

ACOTO

PASSPORT
&
CITIZENSHIP
&
TELEPATHIC DATABASE
OFFICIAL DOCUMENTATION

17 of 36

· A.C.O.T.O. ·

Azurian Confederation Omniversal Treaty Organization

|⌐⌐⌐⌐=⌐⌐⌐⌐=⌐⌐⌐⌐|
|[TRANSLATE]=
|[=[∨]=[3]=[b]=[2]=[1]=[£]
=[↓]=[⊙]=[⊂]=[⅃]=[↓]=[⌐]=[↙]
=[∆]=[7]=[7]=[∇]=[∕]=[0]=[0]=[◊]
=[◆]=[∫]=[[0]=1;[0]=[3]^0.0033]]|]

ACOTO

PASSPORT
&
CITIZENSHIP
&
TELEPATHIC DATABASE

OFFICIAL DOCUMENTATION

12 of 36

A.C.O.T.O.

Azurian Confederation Omniversal
Treaty Organization

|⨀⨀⨀ - ⨀⨀⨀ - ⨀⨀⨀⨀|
[[TRANSLATE]=
|[=[∇]=[△]=[○]=[▽]=[▷]=[◁]=[□]
=[◇]=[◎]=[◁]=[◇]=[○]=[◁]=[▷]=[△]
=[△]=[◎]=[△]=[∇]=[△]=[○]=[○]=[=|
=[•]=[◁]=[[0]=1;[0]=[3]^0.0033]]]

PASSPORT
&
CITIZENSHIP
&
TELEPATHIC DATABANK
OFFICIAL DOCUMENTATION

A.C.O.T.O

Azurian Confederation Omniversal
Treaty Organization

|TTETK1=1⁄026?1=TT1TU0|
{[TRANSLATE]=
|[=[V]=[0]=[6]=[4]=[7]=[7]=[
=[1]=[V]=[4]=[6]=[1]=[5]=[4]=
=[6]=[7]=[V]=[6]=[0]=[6]=[6]
=[•]=[§]=[[0]=1;[0]=[3]^0.0033]]|}

PASSPORT
&
CITIZENSHIP
&
TELEPATHIC DATABASE
OFFICIAL DOCUMENTATION

· A · C · O · T · O ·

Azurian Confederation Omniversal Treaty Organization

[TRANSLATE]=
I=[V]=[5]=[C]=[/]=[]=[]
=[L]=[0]=[C]=[L]=[J]=[]=[L]
=[]=[F]=[]=[\]=[/]=[0]=[0]=[0]
=[•]=[/]=[(0]=1;[0]=[3]^0.0033]|]

ACOTO

PASSPORT
&
CITIZENSHIP
&
TELEPATHIC DATABASE

OFFICIAL DOCUMENTATION

15 of 36

A.C.O.T.O.

Azurian Confederation Omniversal
Treaty Organization

[⌐⊤⌐⊤⌐⌐ = ⅃∪⊼⊼⊦⊤ = ⊤⌐∪⊼∪⊠⌐]
[[TRANSLATE]=
|[=[∨]=[⊠]=[⊡]=[⌐]=[⅂]=[⅃]=[⌐]=[⅃]
=[⅃]=[⊠]=[⅃]=[⅂]=[⊡]=[⅃]=[⌐]=[⅃]
=[⌐]=[⊠]=[⅃]=[∪/]=[0]=[0]=[◦]
=[◦]=[·]=[[0]=1;[0]=[3]^0.0033]|]

███████████████████████████████████
███████████████████████████████████
‡‡⊡█⊡⊡•⊼⊼•⊼⊼⊼•⊼⊼⊠⊤⅃‡⊡⊡⊡◦‡⊼⊠⅃•⌐⊠⌐⊤◦⌐⊠⊠‡⅃◦‡⊡⊠⊡◦⊠⅃◦⊤∪⊼⊤∪⊠⊡◦‡

ACOTO

PASSPORT
&
CITIZENSHIP
&
TELEPATHIC DATABASE

OFFICIAL DOCUMENTATION

16 of 36

A.C.O.T.O.

Azurian Confederation Omniversal Treaty Organization

[[TEXT-TRANS-TITLE]]
[[TRANSLATE]=
[[=[V]=[3]=[O]=[7]=[N]=[]=[C]
=[U]=[M]=[C]=[O]=[]=[]=[]=[L]
=[S]=[M]=[N]=[4]=[4]=[O]=[0]=[•]
=[•]=[•]=[[0]=1;[0]=[3]^0.0033]]]]

ACOTO

PASSPORT
&
CITIZENSHIP
&
TELEPATHIC DATABASE

OFFICIAL DOCUMENTATION

17 of 36

A.C.O.T.O.

Azurian Confederation Omniversal
Treaty Organization

|∏∑≈⊃∘∆∏≈∏∿∐∅∘|
{[TRANSLATE]=
|[=[√]=[⊙]=[↺]=[∆]=[∿]=[∏]=[∆]
=[↻]=[∅]=[∏]=[↻]=[⊙]=[∏]=[∆]
=[∆]=[∏]=[∏]=[√]=[∆]=[⊙]=[⊙]=[∘]
=[∘]=[∘]=[[0]=1;[0]=[3]^0.0033]}]}

ACOTO

PASSPORT
&
CITIZENSHIP
&
TELEPATHIC DATABASE
OFFICIAL DOCUMENTATION

18 of 36

A.C.O.T.O.

Azurian Confederation Omniversal

Treaty Organization

|TTEXT=VOXPT=TTXUEO|
{[TRANSLATE=
|[=[√]=[8]=[□]=[?]=[?]=[□]=[○]
=[]=[⊕]=[⊙]=[U]=[□]=[∪]
=[5]=[?]=[?]=[√]=[□]=[○]=[●]
=[●]=[×]=[{0]=1;[0]=[3]^0.0033}]|}

ACOTO

PASSPORT
&
CITIZENSHIP
&
TELEPATHIC DATABASE

OFFICIAL DOCUMENTATION

19 of 36

A.C.O.T.O.

Azurian Confederation Omniversal
Treaty Organization

[TRANSLATE]=
|[=[∨]=[§]=[○]=[⅃]=[⅂]=[]=[⅃]=
[]=[∅]=[Ɵ]=[∏]=[⎍]=[⅃]=[Ƒ]=[⅃]
=[⅃]=[Ϻ]=[Ⴈ]=[∇]=[∕]=[○]=[○]=[○]
=[●]=[ɼ]=[⟨0⟩=1;⟨0⟩=[3]^0.0033]|]

[TEXT=VOXEL=TEXVOX]

PASSPORT
&
CITIZENSHIP
&
TELEPATHIC DATABASE
OFFICIAL DOCUMENTATION

A.C.O.T.O.

Azurian Confederation Omniversal Treaty Organization

```
[|T|E|C|=|/|O|E|7|=|T|I|/|U|O|]
[[TRANSLATE]
=[|=[V|=[O]=[◇]=[/]=[Ɲ]=[Ɲ]=[◇]
=[Ɲ]=[⦶]=[Ɋ]=[Q]=[L]=[S]=[Ɲ]=[↓]
=[Ø]=[Ɲ|=[/]=[√|=[/]=[Ø]=[◇]=[●]
=[●]=[↓]=[↓]=[[0]=1;[0]=[3]^0.0033]]]
```

░▓█▓░▓█▓░▓█▓░▓█▓░▓█▓░▓█▓░▓█▓░▓█▓░

░▓█▓░▓█▓░▓█▓░▓█▓░▓█▓░▓█▓░

PASSPORT
&
CITIZENSHIP
&
TELEPATHIC DATABASE
OFFICIAL DOCUMENTATION

A.C.O.T.O.

Azurian Confederation Omniversal Treaty Organization

[TRANSLATE]
||[=V]=[?]=[O]=[?]=[?]=[O]=[
=[?]=[O]=[O]=[?]=[?]=[?]=[?]=[?]
=[=?]=[?]=[?]=[?]=[O]=[O]=[o]
=[=]=[=]=[[0]=1;[0]=[3]^0.0033]||]

ACOTO

PASSPORT
&
CITIZENSHIP
&
TELEPATHIC DATABASE
OFFICIAL DOCUMENTATION

22 of 36

·A·C·O·T·O·

Azurian Confederation Omniversal
Treaty Organization

[TRANSLATE]
{{=[V]=[2]=[Ⴑ]=[◌]=[⁄]=[⁊]=[]=[⊏]
=[Ⴑ]=[♡]=[◌]=[⊂]=[Ⴑ]=[]=[]=[⁄]
=[◌]=[⁊]=[Ⴑ]=[∨]=[⁄]=[◌]∑[◌]=[●]
=[●]=[⁄]=[{0]=1;[0]=[3]^0.0033]}}}

ACOTO

PASSPORT
&
CITIZENSHIP
&
TELEPATHIC DATABASE
OFFICIAL DOCUMENTATION

23 of 36

A.C.O.T.O.

Azurian Confederation Omniversal Treaty Organization

[⏃⏁⏁⟒⊼⏁⋮⟟⍜⋔⟟⟒⟒⍀⏁⟟⟒⎐⟒⏃⟒⏃]
[[TRANSLATE]=
|[=[V]=[3]=[⏃]=[⏃]=[⍀]=[⏁]=[⟒]
=[⏁]=[⎍]=[⟟]=[⏃]=[⏁]=[⟒]=[⏃]
=[⏃]=[⍙]=[⏃]=[⋔]=[⌿]=[⍜]=[⍜]=[⍜]
=[⍜]=[⍀]=[⌖]=[[⍜]=1;[⍜]=[⌖]^0.0033]]|]

ACOTO

PASSPORT
&
CITIZENSHIP
&
TELEPATHIC DATABASE

OFFICIAL DOCUMENTATION

24 of 36

A.C.O.T.O.

Azurian Confederation Omniversal Treaty Organization

|=[][][=]=[][]=[][]=[]=[][][=]
[[TRANSLATE]=
[[=[V]=[2]=[5]=[2]=[2]=[7]=[1]=[2]
[7]=[V]=[2]=[1]=[2]=[5]=[7]=[4]
=[5]=[7]=[2]=[1]=[4]=[0]=[0]=[0]
=[•]=[•]=[1]=[[0]=1;[0]=[3]^0.0033]]]

36

ACOTO

PASSPORT
&
CITIZENSHIP
&
TELEPATHIC DATABASE
OFFICIAL DOCUMENTATION

25 of 36

A.C.O.T.O.

Azurian Confederation Omniversal Treaty Organization

[[TRANSLATE]=
[[=[∇]=[§]=[○]=[♢]=[?]=[ ]=[ ]
=[ ]=[ ]=[ ]=[ ]=[ ]=[ ]=[ ]
=[ ]=[?]=[ ]=[√]=[ ]=[○]=[○]=[○]
=[●]=[◊]=[[0]=1;[0]=[3]^0.0033]]]

ACOTO

PASSPORT
&
CITIZENSHIP
&
TELEPATHIC DATABASE
OFFICIAL DOCUMENTATION

26 of 36

A.C.O.T.O.

Azurian Confederation Omniversal Treaty Organization

[[TRANSLATE]=
|[=[V]=[B]=[U]=[C]=[P]=[7]=[T]=[E]
=[L]=[M]=[K]=[S]=[U]=[E]=[T]=[L]
=[B]=[M]=[Z]=[4]=[2]=[0]=[0]=[e]
=[e]=[r]=[[0]=1;[0]=[3]^0.0033]|]

ACOTO

PASSPORT
&
CITIZENSHIP
&
TELEPATHIC DATABASE
OFFICIAL DOCUMENTATION

27 of 36

A.C.O.T.O.

Azurian Confederation Omniversal Treaty Organization

[⌐⊥⊏⌐=⌐⊐⊏⊐⊏=⊏⊥⊐⊏⊐]
[[TRANSLATE]=
|[=(∨)=[2]=[b]=[⊐]=[⌐]=[⌐]=[⌐]
=[⊔]=[⊗]=[⊓]=[⊔]=[⊓]=[⊔]
=[⊐]=[⊓]=[⊓]=[∧]=[0]=[0]=[0]
=[●]=[⌐]=[0]=1;[0]=[3]^0.0033}} |]

OFFICIAL DOCUMENTATION

A.C.O.T.O.

Azurian Confederation Omniversal

Treaty Organization

[⌂⍜⌰⎈ - ⎁⍜⌰⌿⎁ - ⏀⎁⌰⏃⌾⍜]
[[TRANSLATE]=
[[=[∨]=[8]=[○]=[□]=[♢]=[▽]=[□]=[□]
=[▽]=[⊙]=[□]=[♢]=[▽]=[□]=[□]=[△]
=[♢]=[♡]=[▽]=[♢]=[▽]=[○]=[○]=[●]
=[•]=[♦]=[[0]=1;[0]=[3]^0.0033]]]

⚠ANTI-FRAUD⚠

ACOTO

PASSPORT
&
CITIZENSHIP
&
TELEPATHIC DATABANK
OFFICIAL DOCUMENTATION

29 of 36

A.C.O.T.O.

Azurian Confederation Omniversal
Treaty Organization

[|⊤|⊥|⊼|=⌐⋁⋀⋂⋔⌐=⊤⋁∨⋃⋓]
[[TRANSLATE]=
[[=[∨]=[⊙]=[⊙]=[∇]=[⊳]=[⊓]=[∠]
=[⊔]=[⋈]=[⊲]=[⊓]=[⊔]=[⊓]=[⊓]=[∠]
=[⋈]=[⊓]=[⊓]=[√]=[∠]=[⊙]=[⊙]=[•]
=[•]=[∘]=[[0]=1;[0]=[3]^0.0033]|]

ACOTO

PASSPORT
&
CITIZENSHIP
&
TELEPATHIC DATABASE

OFFICIAL DOCUMENTATION

30 of 36

A.C.O.T.O.

Azurian Confederation Omniversal
Treaty Organization

[TEXT-VOYPI-TIXUOI]
[[TRANSLATE]=
|[=(V)=(B)=(b)=(.)=(/)=(7)=(l)=(C)
=(l)=(0)=(K)=(l)=(l)=(P)=(l)=(L)
=(B)=(M)=(R)=(V)=(O)=(o)=(o)
=(•)=(×)=[(0)=1;(0)=(3)^0.0033]}|]

ACOTO

PASSPORT
&
CITIZENSHIP
&
TELEPATHIC DATABANK
OFFICIAL DOCUMENTATION

37 of 36

A.C.O.T.O.

Azurian Confederation Omniversal Treaty Organization

|TIZKT=VOXXPI=TIZXVMO|
|TRANSLATE|=
|[=(V)=[S]=[0]=[C]=[Z]=[Y]=[1]=[C]
=[1]=[M]=[Q]=[I]=[U]=[C]=[T]=[J]
=[B]=[M]=[A]=[V]=[J]=[O]=[0]=[0]
=[•]=[J]=[0]=1;[0]=[3]^0.0033}||

ACOTO

PASSPORT
&
CITIZENSHIP
&
TELEPATHIC DATABASE
OFFICIAL DOCUMENTATION

32 of 36

A.C.O.T.O.

Azurian Confederation Omniversal Treaty Organization

[|∏∃∑]=⅂⋀⊘&⅁⅂=∏∑∏⊔⊘]
[[TRANSLATE]=
[[=[⋁=⊟=⅄=⊠=⅂=⅂=⅂
=⅄=⋔=⊠=⊟=⊔=⅂=⅂=⅃
=⅂=⅀=⅁=⅂=⅂=⊙=⊙=⊙]
=[•]=[•]=[[0]=1;[0]=[3]^0.0033]}]]

ACOTO

PASSPORT
&
CITIZENSHIP
&
TELEPATHIC DATABASE

OFFICIAL DOCUMENTATION

33 of 36

A.C.O.T.O.

Azurian Confederation Omniversal
Treaty Organization

[TRANSLATE]=
[[=|V|=[8]=[0]=[4]=[7]=[N]=[]=[]
=[4]=[6]=[4]=[4]=[M]=[]=[T]=[4]
=[]=[7]=[4]=[4]=[4]=[0]=[0]=[0]
=[◦]=[◦]=[[0]=1;[0]=[3]^0.0033]]|]

ACOTO

PASSPORT
&
CITIZENSHIP
&
TELEPATHIC DATABASE

OFFICIAL DOCUMENTATION

34 of 36

A.C.O.T.O.

Azurian Confederation Omniversal
Treaty Organization

[[TE][T]-[/0][0][T]-[T][T][00]]
[[TRANSLATE]=
|[=[V]=[9]=[b]=[2]-[7]=[7]-[C]
=[1]=[0]=[2]=[0]=[1]=[0]=[L]
=[8]=[7]=[7]=[U]=[/]=[0]=[0]=[e]
=[e]=[/]=[[0]=1;[0]=[3]^0.0033]]|]

ACOTO

PASSPORT
&
CITIZENSHIP
&
TELEPATHIC DATABASE

OFFICIAL DOCUMENTATION

35 of 36

|||PROTOCOL_LOOP--[SELF_IDENTITY_A.C.O.T.O._PASSPORT_WHOLE=||0
||0|=CL/:/LC;||||

A.C.O.T.O.

Azurian Confederation Omniversal
Treaty Organization

|]\/[]]\[]=]\/0&?]= T\\/[\0|
[[TRANSLATE]=
|[=|\/]=[8]=[\]=[\]=[/]=[/]=[\]=[\]
=[\]=[0]=[\]=[\]=[\]=[\]
=[\]=[?]=[\]=[\/]=[0]=[0]=[0]
=[0]=[·]=[x]=[[0]=1;[0]=[3]^0.0033]||]

ACOTO

PASSPORT
&
CITIZENSHIP
&
TELEPATHIC DATABASE

OFFICIAL DOCUMENTATION

36 of 36

A.C.O.T.O.

Azurian Confederation Omniversal Treaty Organization

[[] []=[] = []/[]&[] = []/[]/[]]
[[TRANSLATE]=
[[=[V]=[]=[©]=[8]=[7]=[]=[]=[2
=[]=[M]=[]=[]=[8]=[]=[]=[]=[4
=[]=[]=[M]=[4]=[L]=[0]=[0]=[8]
=[8]=[8]=[[0]=1;[0]=[3]^0.0033]]]]